SWEETHEARTS & VALENTINE

To dear Maria
Love from
Mummy.

Hope you have a lovely
Valentines day
1983

SWEETHEARTS & VALENTINES

TRUE LOVE FADETH NEVER

Judith Holder

Webb&Bower
EXETER, ENGLAND

Published in Great Britain 1980 by
Webb & Bower (Publishers) Limited,
33 Southernhay East, Exeter, Devon, EX1 1NS

Distributed by WHS Distributors
(a division of W. H. Smith and Son Limited)
Euston Street, Freeman's Common, Aylestone Road,
Leicester, LE2 7SS

Designed by Peter Wrigley

© Webb & Bower (Publishers) Limited 1980

British Library Cataloguing in Publication Data
Holder, Judith
    Sweethearts and Valentines
    1. Valentines – Pictorial works
    I. Title
    769'.5   NC1866. V3

    ISBN 0–906671–03–5

Typeset in Great Britain
by Filmtype Services Limited

Printed and bound in Hong Kong
by Mandarin Publishers Limited

INTRODUCTION

The custom of sending cards or tokens of one's love to one's sweetheart on St Valentine's Day, the 14th of February, goes back to pagan times and certainly long before 270AD, when Valentine, a priest in Rome, was beaten and executed for his Christian faith. A church was built to his memory near the Porta del Papolo, a gate to the city which was at one time known as Porta Valentini. Valentine himself was an epileptic, and after his death fellow-sufferers believed he would take a particular interest in them and intercede on their behalf; in parts of Germany epilepsy was known as St Valentine's sickness. But this, of course, has nothing to do with sweethearts and true love, his association with lovers being accidental.

The association of love with St Valentine's day came about because of the Roman feast of Lupercalia. This important feast was one of respect for Pan, one of whose tasks it was to drive the wolves away from the flocks. During the ceremony a sacrifice of goats and a dog would be made. The foreheads of two young boys would be stained with the blood from the sacrifice, the skins of the goats would be cut into strips, and then the boys would run through the streets lashing everyone they met with bundles of these strips. Young women took care not to avoid the lashes, as they believed that being struck by them would assist conception of a child.

This festival – as well as, of course, many others – was introduced to Britain during the Roman occupation, and became the Spring Festival held on the 15th of February.

The early Christian missionaries and priests tried to do away with pagan customs and superstitions such as this festival, attempting to substitute saints' days for them; thus Saint Valentine, who was killed on the eve of Lupercalia, was introduced. St Valentine's Day thus now perpetuates the memory of the Spring Festival, the season when birds mate and "a young man's fancy lightly turns to thoughts of love".

As early as the fifteenth century the custom became popular whereby the young would on St Valentine's Day choose by lot – drawing names from a box – lovers, sweethearts, or just special friends for the ensuing year; the owner of the name drawn in the lottery would be sent a present of some kind by the person who had drawn the name. The gifts could be expensive ones, as Samuel Pepys recorded in his diary, and were generally accompanied by mottoes. Over the centuries these gifts-with-mottoes became cards containing verses, mottoes, and even puzzles.

By the eighteenth century expensive presents were no longer expected, a token or letter taking their place. The transition from this stage to the modern practice of sending a card on St Valentine's Day to express one's true love for one's sweetheart is easy to imagine.

An early precursor of the valentine card with its motto was the true-love knot. This was an elaborately created design around which was written a message such that one could choose a line at random and then read the message to the end: the effect is rather as if one took the strips of paper from a modern telegram and pasted them down onto a flat

sheet of paper in such a way that the end result resembled a knotted length of string. A message from one of the early seventeenth-century cards reads: "True love is a pretious pleasure, Rich delight unvalud treasure, Two firme heartes in one meeting, Grasping hand in hand ne'r fleeting, Wreathlike like a maze entwineing, Two faire mindes in one combineing; Foe to faithless vowes perfidious, True love is a knott religious, Dead the sinnes and falmeing rise, Through beauties soule reduceing eyes, Deafe to gold enchaunting witches, Love for vertue not for riches, Such is true loves boundless measure, True love is a pretious pleasure."

Most of the cards shown in this book are Victorian, and so perhaps it is worth talking for just a moment about how they were made. Today we generally simply buy a card from the store and send it, but during the nineteenth century things were not always as easy as that. Some of the cards shown here were purchased in the form of their various components and actually assembled by their senders: thus one might purchase the blank card, a paper lace frame, a picture or pictures, and a verse or motto, then glue all these together to produce one's own specially designed valentine. It is particularly romantic to think of young Victorian gentlemen, who would rarely lift a finger in practical matters such as sewing or cooking, spending hours with scissors and paste assembling these valentines.

But enough of the history. Let me now release you to wander through that magic land of love, the country of the valentine.

FORGET-ME-NOT

This little gem of azure hue,
  Is full of interest to me,
Because, my love, it tells of you,
  In silent language, clear and free.
Its modest bloom in such a spot,
  In hue it's kindred to the sky,
Confirm the sweet Forget-me-not,
  The flower of Hope and Constancy.

This tiny valentine of lace paper is only two and a half inches across and yet has survived in good condition for nearly a century and a half. Almost certainly it was originally mounted on card.

The two illustrations embossed in the paper are of, on the left, a young couple, and, on the right, a church, so that it seems certain that this was a valentine sent by a young man to his betrothed. This view would seem to be supported by the tenor of the verse, which certainly would be inappropriate were he merely one of many distant, and anonymous, admirers.

The forget-me-not is the flower of constancy and faithfulness in the Language of Flowers, a language in which each flower was ascribed a special meaning. Although some flowers have had such meanings for millennia, it was only from about the 1840s that "complete" systems became popular: in the demure Victorian age, secret passions could therefore best be expressed in the form of a bouquet, each plant of which possessed hidden meaning.

Forget-me-not.

This little gem of azure hue,
Is full of interest to me,
Because, my love, it tells of you,
In silent language, clear and free.
Its modest bloom in such a spot,
In hue it's kindred to the sky,
Confirm the sweet Forget-
me-not,
The flower of Hope and
Constancy.

BIRTH OF LOVE

Love – it is the gift of Heaven,
Like the rose, how sweet its bloom,
And where'er is felt its presence,
There it dissipates each gloom.
And the heart that loveth truly,
In its first affection pure,
Shall, as long as life continues,
Find its happiness endure.

LOVE AMONGST THE ROSES

Though the rose scent dies and the
   rose decays
The rose of the spirit never is sere;
Soft as roses be all thy ways,
And thou, may'st thou through all
   thy days,
Open and greaten, even as these,
Petal by petal and year by year.

The motto'd ring, the riband fair,
Accept my Valentine;
They come from one who loves you
true,
Whose faithful heart is thine.

This is a very early valentine: the watermark of the paper is 1808, and for various other reasons it seems likely that it was sent to its lucky recipient in 1811. It was clearly painted by hand, probably in inks, and the loving care that went into its preparation is obvious. To the left of the main part of the picture is a wedding ring, and to the right is a riband bearing simply the word "Valentine". What is less easy to understand is the message at the base of the main part of the picture. This reads: "mjsae dfdobre. son." One can only conclude that it must be in some secret lovers' code, possibly based on Latin. Indeed an effective secret code, for now we may never know the loving message it conveyed.

We see here also the heart pierced by Cupid's arrows, the symbol of true love that for centuries has expressed passions, whether in the form of a valentine, as here, or carved into the trunk of a tree at some trysting place, or longed-for trysting place: we know that in this case the sender's love was indeed returned.

The message inscribed within the blue diamond is clear and simple. It reads: "Love the Giver." But there is yet another message in this charmingly crafted valentine, written around the pink ring:

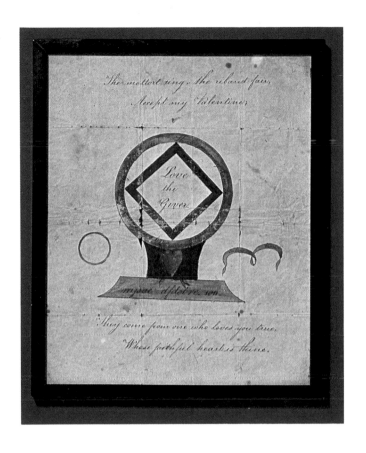

My sweet and charming Valentine
That you may have each wish of mine.

ONE SHORT HOUR

The wandering winds,
*   that seem no law to know*
Scatter the seeds of many
*   a precious flower*
And this our love,
*   rooted I trust to grow,*
Was sown by chance,
*   and sprang in one short hour.*

This verse from a valentine of the 1870s seems apt to complement these silk embroidered cards, manufactured in France and used by Allied troops in WWI to write home to their loved ones. The inscription on the back of the centre card sums up so many of the stories behind them all. It reads: "Dearest Wife, Just a card of a few lines hoping you will like it. You will think I am in an awful muddle over the letters and I expect you will be getting tired of me telling you that I have not received one yet. I hope you have got a letter off to me addressed to R.E. Base No 10 Company Sp. Brigade B.E.F. as I look like being here a bit longer, so I am sorry I sent you that other card telling you not to write here. Anyway, dear, you can chance one, as I shall get it some time. It is rotten not hearing from you for so long and I know it will be troubling you, but cheer up old dear, otherwise I am all right and I sincerely hope you and the kiddies are the same. Now dear that's all this time so I will close with fondest love and kind thoughts to you and kiddies.xxxxxxxxxxxx"

Absent yet ever near

My heart's
greeting

TO MY DEAR WIFE

Forget Me Not

May constancy all
doubt repel
And joy betoken
where we dwell

This is a very beautiful valentine and, to judge by the verse upon it, must have been given to a husband by his wife, or to a wife by her husband. The bouquet of flowers is exquisitely printed on fine tissue paper with a delicacy that must have been hard to achieve: it contains a rose, the symbol of true love; a pansy, symbolizing "thoughts"; and of course forget-me-nots.

I have culled a little flower,
My messenger to be;
Let it whisper in thine ear
All I would say to thee.

This silver-paper lace card must have delighted the heart of the young lady who received it. Behind the central picture, which is of roses, forget-me-nots and daisies (the daisy denotes "innocence"), there is a perfumed pad. The whole construction is contained within an elaborately decorated box.

On the inside of the lid her eye must have fallen at once on the verse, which is surrounded by pansies and forget-me-nots. Beside it sits a despairing Cupid, head in hand, looking disconsolately at a heart which his arrow has pierced. Let us hope that this valentine won over the fair lady where Cupid himself had failed.

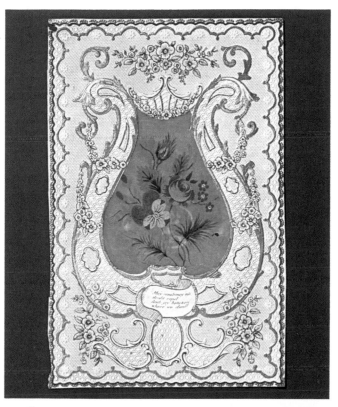

TO MY VALENTINE
Tell me, Sweet,
does that heart of thine
Cherish a thought
that is hope to mine?

Among these cards we can find all the most popular ingredients for the declaration of true love. There are pairs of hearts pierced by arrows from Cupid's bow, roses to show that love is true, forget-me-nots, a white dove of purity, and, on one of the cards, an engagement ring. Two of the cards bear cherubs.

This elaborately crafted valentine must have delighted the lady who received it from her husband. The front is of delicate paper lace. Two bouquets of flowers, made in cotton, lie to either side of the frame; they rather obscure a pair of pastoral figures which are embossed into the paper. To the left, and almost completely covered, is the figure of a woman bearing a sheaf of wheat; to the right is that of a man, bearing not only a wheat-sheaf but also a scythe.

None here are happy but in part
Full bliss were bliss divine,
There dwells some wish
    in ev'ry heart
And doubtless one in thine.

This is an extremely ornate card of lace paper with highly intricate designs representing church windows and arches. In the centre arch, above the coloured picture, stand two angels embracing, watched by two cherubs, one of whom is carrying the bow and quiver that identify him as Cupid. In the arches to either side of the coloured picture are female figures. The arch motif is continued in the embossing of the back part of the card, which serves almost as a frame for the front part.

Across the central part of the card there is stretched extremely fine tissue paper, to which have been glued little silvery motifs. The coloured picture, a tiny one of a figure playing a pipe of some kind, is also glued to the tissue paper, although the blue ground on which he stands has been touched in by hand, probably in watercolour.

The sender of the card was not content merely with the poem printed on the front: inside is a handwritten message which reads:

If you love me
    as I love you
Nothing but death
    shall part us two.

For dear Annie   With M. J.'s love

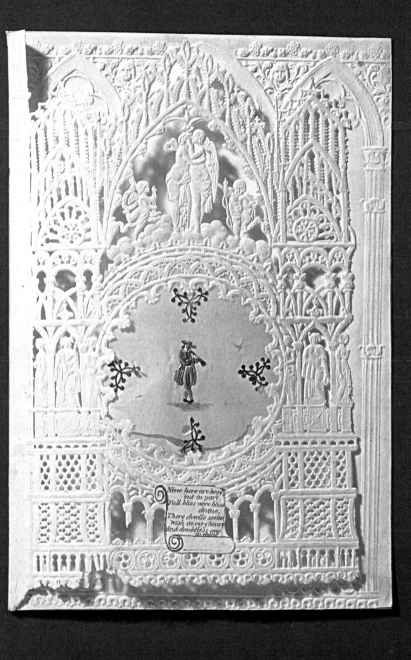

None here are happy
but in part,
Full bliss were bliss
divine,
There dwells some
wish in every heart
And doubtless so in thine.

The valentine above was posted to Mary Ann Sherriff in 1832 "from your ever faithful Arthur".

We can imagine how delighted Mary Ann must have been when she received it, and she would have had no doubts of Arthur's feelings towards her as on the front are hand-painted flowers, roses and lilac. The rose denotes the declaration of true love and the lilac the first dawning emotions of such true love. Her delight must have increased yet further when she found a thread among the flowers: as she pulled it she saw revealed a cupid with bow and arrows encircled by a yellow band and the words: "Thus may the archer turn on thee, those arms of love which conquered me." Perhaps we can hope that by St Valentine's Day 1833 Mary Ann was wearing Arthur's ring.

Opposite we see a similar, rather later, "bee-hive" card in both closed and open conditions.

Condemn me not in seeking to impart
In these few lines the secret of my heart.
To thee I own.

(What I've essayed, but never could reveal
But by this Valentine:) the Love I feel
For you alone.

Here are two valentines of a once very popular style, taking the form of cheques or banknotes drawn upon the "Bank of Love" or some other similar institution. The upper valentine is from the USA, probably New York; the lower is from the "Temple of Hymen", is British.

It is little remembered today, but there was during the closing decades of the eighteenth century an extremely popular establishment in London called the Temple of Hymen. It was run by the eccentric Scots quack Dr James Graham (unlike many of his colleagues, Graham was actually entitled to his "Dr"), and featured many strange and mysterious wonders the very touching or seeing of which could be guaranteed to ease young lovers' paths to happiness. There were of course financial strings attached – and the notes were drawn upon the Bank of England, not that of Love! – and at the height of its popularity the Temple of Hymen was to bring Graham sums which even today seem impressive. But his establishment was long gone when this note was issued.

Each side of this unusual valentine bears a bouquet of roses and a loving verse. The card is decorated with a white fringe of silk. But what makes it so unusual is that the two sides of the valentine are connected with cotton so that the card as a whole may be opened up much like a lady's handbag – did the sender slip his message of adoration into this pocket?

May with its charms, brings not a flower,
April sends not its balmy shower,
Refreshing though their sweets may be,
Yet sweeter far they smells to me:
Thou sweetest flower, to my fond heart,
Oh all my hopes the pride,
The sacred altar soon will see
In thee, my blushing bride.

The bride-to-be must have been charmed by this
exquisite hand-coloured card with its loving message. The border is of very finely perforated paper
lace, and the pictures, which are quite delicately
treated, show almost as clearly as the verse that this
card was given by a young man to his fiancée not
long before their intended marriage. This card
would seem to augur that it would be a happy one.

This is a threefold card of paper lace painted with silver and gold. It has the verse on one of its six faces and flowers on the others. Here we can see, on the left, a bouquet of red roses, which denote true love, as always. In the centre, there is another rose, of paper glued to padded silver velvet. The lilies-of-the-valley describe, in the Language of Flowers, a "return to happiness"; behind the picture of them we can just see a charming illustration of a young girl chasing a butterfly. On the three sides that we cannot see there are, apart from the verse, a generous vaseful of forget-me-nots and a mixed bouquet. The young man who received this elaborate card must have treasured it long after St Valentine's Day, especially since the velvet pad would have been sprinkled with perfume, to bring her even closer to his thoughts at all times.

UNDYING LOVE

My heart and soul shall be thine,
Come what may come of ills the
  worst,
As faithful to thy life's decline
 As when they wooed and loved thee
  first.

Then hear, dear love, my heart's
  true vow,
 And let thy heart confide in me;
I will not change — my love
  shall grow
 Till we in wedlock's bands shall be.

BIRTHDAY

This is the birthday of my Love,
  Then vanish care and sorrow;
To-day shall mirth and pleasure reign,
  Tho' grief should come tomorrow.
My Love draws near with airy tread,
  And glances shy and sweet;
Sing, little birds, above her head,
  Bloom, flowers, beneath her feet.

This is a delightful birthday card that must have given supreme pleasure to its recipient. the paper lace is coloured a bright blue, in striking contrast

to most other cards sent by the Victorians to their sweethearts; it has also been gilded. Its perforations are tremendously intricate. And on the inside, when she opened it, the young lady found another piece of delicately patterned paper lace, with the loving verse and coloured flowers; behind the embossed golden roses she could see, just peeping out, the pale pink perfume sachet.

The valentine above is a very delicate card, made of paper lace and pink net and decorated with silver motifs and two paper hearts. The hearts are encircled by roses: the one on the left has wild dog roses surrounding it, the one on the right cultivated garden roses. At the top of each heart is a blazing torch. As we can see, the left-hand heart contains simply the word "Love" while the one on the right has a little flying Cupid – alas, now without a head. Above the hearts flies a dove bearing the message of love; and on the riband beneath the hearts the sender has written: "Bid me hope."

The inscription inside the card is a little enigmatic. It reads: "Mary Clarke 1859." Later the same person has added: "To Oliver." We can but guess as to why either Mary or Oliver should have written thus, so let us merely hope that they found joy with each other.

The smaller card beneath has pasted to it some lovely roses printed on embossed paper. Beneath these sits a small plump cherub holding up the message: "I love to think on thee." The poem handwritten inside the card reads:

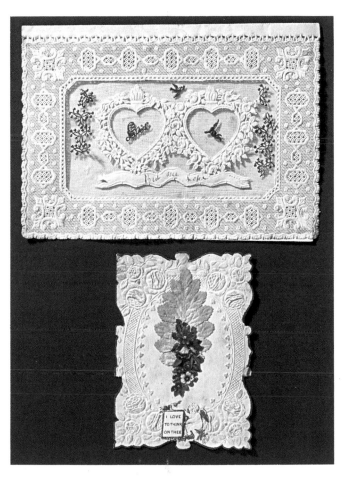

I LOVE TO THINK ON THEE

*If you love me
As I love you
Naught but death
Shall part us two.*

Some wed for gold and some for
   pleasure,
And some wed only at their leisure,
But if you wish to wait and weep,
When e'er you wed,
   look well before you leap.

And the picture, revealed when the hoop is raised, warns the young man only too well one of the possible perils of marriage!

It may seem strange, looking back a century later, that not all of the valentines the Victorians sent were by any means expressing the sentiments of true love. There was a tremendous vogue for vulgar and sometimes genuinely spiteful cards. The comic valentine is, of course, still with us today, but no modern lover would expect to receive on the 14th of February a card from the "other girl" telling her that she was a snake in the grass or insulting her appearance. Yet, however bizarre it may seem to us now, in the late nineteenth century it was not at all an uncommon occurrence.

But this card seems to belong to yet another class, for it does not seem to advise the young man to think deeply about his feeling for his true love, as one might expect were it from a rejected rival, but instead to warn him about the dangers of falling too deeply in love with *any* woman. Perhaps it was designed to be sent from parent to child, or from best friend to best friend, to suggest that he pause for serious consideration before dashing too rashly into marriage.

FOR *A* FRIEND

Have communion with few,
Be familiar with one.
Deal gently of many,
Speak evil of none.

It is a litle hard to guess whether this charming card
was originally intended as a valentine or as a
birthday greeting for a child, but no one can doubt
that it was given with great love. The front of the
card, which one cannot see when the card is opened
as it is here, shows the figure of a boy holding a
single red rose and framed by a wreath of yellow
and pink roses; beneath him is another wreath, this
time of forget-me-nots, bearing the legend: "To
my little pet."

Upon this day one secret of my heart,
  Till now concealed, shall truly be
    confessed.
If there's a youth whose love
  I would command,
To whom resign my maiden heart
    and hand:
  You are that youth to whose oft
    proferred vow,
Of Love and Constancy I answer now;
  If still unchanged for me alone you live,
Let your reply that fond assurance give.

This extremely attractive hand-coloured card, printed in sepia, shows a bluebird bringing this fond message of love to a sailor – who, we must hope, was delighted with the maiden's declaration of love for him, and comforted by the knowledge that at the end of his long voyage she would be waiting for him. And a very long voyage it might be, for this card was sent in about 1840, when a sailor might be away from port for several years.

The hand-colouring must almost certainly have been done, not by the sender, but by the card's manufacturer, for in places it is quite crude. But this was in an age when hand-colouring was at its height.

We should note that in the first half of the nineteenth century valentines showing soldiers and sailors were extremely popular, owing to the turbulent nature of the early decades.

Upon this day one secret of my breast
Till now concealed, shall truly be confessed.
If there's a youth whose love I would command,
To whom resign my maiden heart & hand;
You are that youth to whose off proffered vow,
Of Love and Constancy I answer now.
If still unchanged for me alone you live,
Let your reply that fond assurance give.

REMEMBRANCE

In pleasure's dream, or sorrow's hour
In crowded hall, or lonely bower,
The business of my soul shall be
For ever to remember thee.

This card is designed to express true love not on St Valentine's day, the 14th of February, but at Christmas, as is made clear by the robin redbreast with holly leaves and berries; holly is represented in the Language of Flowers as "foresight".

The main body of the card is of intricately embossed paper, the portrait of the girl also being embossed and glued to it. The verse inside the card, "Remembrance", is on a separately printed slip of paper and has been glued into place, obviously by the sender. It is clear that, in his selection of this verse, there lies a hidden love story.

My love is ever with me
In dreams by night or day; –
Go, gentle flowers and whisper
"Forget-me-not, I pray."

This beautiful valentine, dating from about the 1860s or 1870s, is made up of three layers separated by cardboard hinges. The layer in the foreground is of woven silk and shows a nosegay of forget-me-nots, the flower of faithfulness, with the words "True Love Fadeth Never". On the second layer are three pansies (originally four) of paper glued to silk: the pansy is, of course, the flower of thoughts.

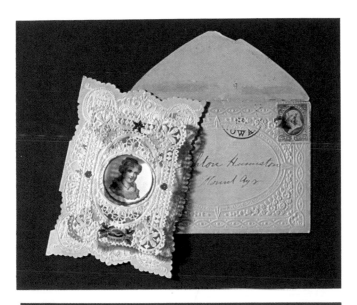

TO MY VALENTINE

Oh! please to be my Valentine,
See my love is worn and thin.
He's worked with me so very hard,
To try your heart to win.

These three cards, all North American and sent between 1909 and 1912, show three variations on the theme of the heart being pierced by an arrow from Cupid's quiver.

Cupid was the Roman equivalent of the Greek god Eros; he was originally regarded as a primaeval god, born out of Chaos, but later regarded by the Greeks as the son of Aphrodite, goddess of beauty and sexual love; according to various traditions, his father was Hermes, Ares or even Zeus himself. His status as god of passion was gradually eroded, until he became a chubby little winged infant, just as is the Cupid we see in two of these cards.

The Roman view of Cupid also varied: to some he was the beautiful winged youth that Eros had once been; to others he was the mischievous flying infant who fired arrows of passion into the hearts of those who were to fall in love.

The lowest of these three cards carries a simple embossed verse:

Love, dear little artist – superfine,
Painted your picture for my
Valentine.

Love's
Fair
Exchange.

To My
Valentine

Oh! please to be
my Valentine.
See love is
worn and thin.
He's worked with me
so very hard,
To try your
heart to win.

THE ROSE

The rose will cease to blow,
The eagle turn a dove,
The stream will cease to flow,
Ere I will cease to love.

The sun will cease to shine,
The world will cease to move,
The stars their light resign,
Ere I will cease to love.

PURE LOVE

Long in secret I have sighed, –
For you all others I've denied,
And if your heart I cannot gain,
I ne'er will wed another swain.
Pray my love an answer send,
And let it be in honour penn'd,
That I may no longer languish,
And soon, oh soon relieve my anguish.

Lucky the man who received this card, inside which was a paper pad soaked in perfume. Having lifted the flowered part of the card forward to read the verse, printed on silk, he could then read beneath the flowers further symbols of his love's intent: "Joy", "Peace", "Prosperity", "Health", "Happiness" and "Success".

Today, without seeing you,
  my time has hung heavily.
It was sad, alas,
  without my heart's delight.
 ୨ଧ୨ଧ୨ଧ
My poor loving heart
  waited this morning,
But it could not see you.
  Will you be here tomorrow?
 ୨ଧ୨ଧ୨ଧ
Yes, because always
  my heart will beat for you,
Or even it will die at your feet.
 ୨ଧ୨ଧ୨ଧ
My soul is enslaved
  by your potent charms.
My love will endure
  my whole life long.

These four French cards – the verses above are a rather free translation of the verses on them – are part of a set of six which, when laid out together, show the arrow flying in full circle. The six cards seem to have been sent to the same man, M. André Geoffre of Poitiers, on successive days, and the messages on the back of them tell a rather sad tale. The early cards carry messages expressing true love and utmost affection, but the later ones become more pleading until the last says simply:
"Vous n'êtes pas gentil."

Love's stratagem – to plead the vow
  Of joy supreme.
Of bliss in rapture's words to show,
  As in a dream.

This beautiful card is one of a set of fourteen – a valentine's dozen – called "The Despondent Lover". No girl could be unmoved by the exquisite border of stylized flowers – roses for love, columbine representing folly, forget-me-nots – and butterflies, or by the hand-coloured centre panel surrounded by flowers, turtledoves and swans.

Think kindly of the erring one –
  Ye know not of the power
With which the dark temptation came
  In some unguarded hour.
Forget not thou hast often sinned
  And sinful yet may be;
Deal gently with the erring one,
  As God has dealt with thee.

This extraordinary rhyme was posted in London on the 13th of February 1864 to Miss Mary Turner in Northwich. It is mounted on lace paper card which shows a church at the top and, at the bottom, a couple standing by a house with a gate and a horse in a field. The front layer is again of lace paper, coloured with silver and gold and embossed with shells.

Whatever in the
chequer'd scene
Of life may be my lot,
Believe me, I shall happy be
If you forget me not.

This valentine was posted to Miss Elizabeth Petty
of New York near Harrogate, England. At first it
may seem surprising that so fragile and complexly
delicate a valentine has survived the rigours of
over a century, even despite the box in which it
came; but we should remember that Elizabeth's
suitor must have felt her to be a very special person
indeed if he went to the considerable trouble of
giving her a card of this extravagance. We must
hope that his feelings were returned.

If I, in verse, thy worth rehearse,
Have pity on each line:
Oh charming maid, pray don't
upbraid
Thy constant Valentine.

This valentine dates from about the 1840s and is on thin paper of double quarto size. Many early nineteenth-century valentines were so printed, for they were posted in the days before the introduction of the envelope, or at least before the envelope became universally popular. The valentine would be folded up and sealed with sealing-wax; the loved one would prise this open to find within not only a verse such as this but also handwritten messages from her young hopeful.

My dear i rite you
just a line and
wish you a happy
valentine though
valentine is over
do not say i am
to late for if you
do i am afaered
my heart will
nearly break
Take this and read
it and except it from
me it came from
the one that love the
i love the wilt
thou love me
i wonder wich love best for
your love i can
not spell so
you must guse
the rest but
if you will be
mine i will
be thine and
so good morrow
valentine

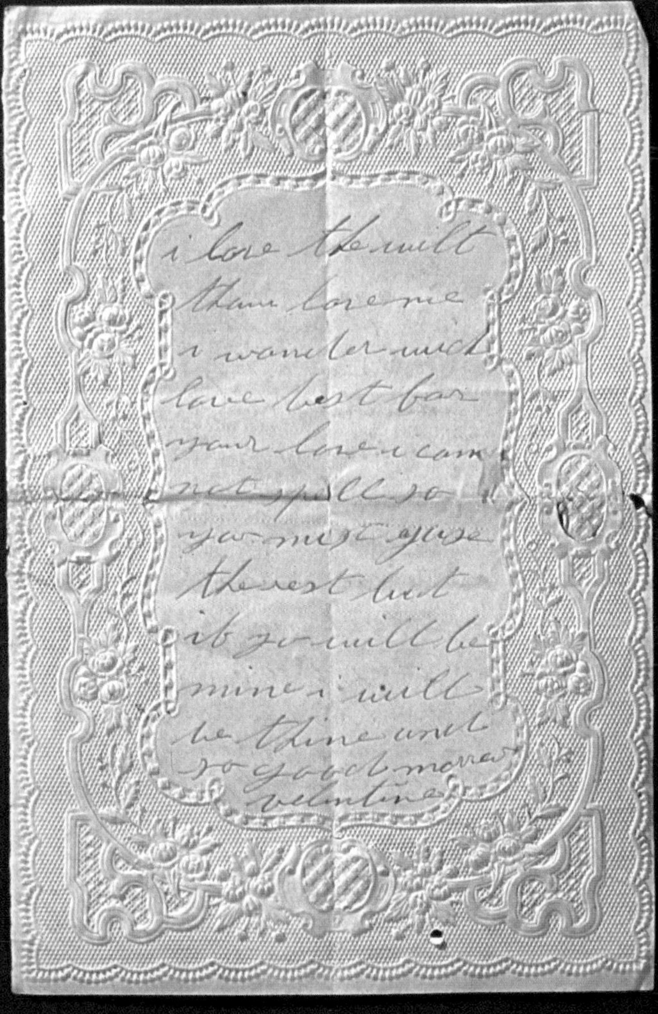

i love the will
thine love me
i wonder much
love best bar
your love i can
not spell so
you must guess
the rest but
if you will be
mine i will
be thine and
so good morrow
valentine

Each has the power to wound, but he
    Who wounds that he may witness pain,
Has learnt no law of charity,
    Which ne'er inflicts a pang in
      vain,
'Tis Godlike to awaken joy,
    Or sorrow's influence to subdue,
But not to wound, nor to annoy,
    Is part of virtue's lessons too.

This is an astonishing card indeed. The very sorrowful, almost bitter, reproach of the verse, which is excellently printed on silk, comes within a card of outstanding elegance. The paper lace is of exquisite intricacy and depicts roses, the flowers of true love, and the lyre shapes so frequently found on Victorian valentines. The picture of fuchsias at the front of the card has been painted *by hand*, almost certainly by the sender of the card, and in the Language of Flowers the fuchsia symbolizes "taste" or "elegance", a quality which hardly matches the recriminatory tones of the verse.

It would seem likely that the young lady who sent this card purchased the backing and the two sheets of paper lace separately, and made the valentine from them. We shall never know what ran through her mind as she did so, nor what it was that the young man had done to deserve so unpleasant a surprise on the morning of St Valentine's Day, but we can hope that at last they were reunited.

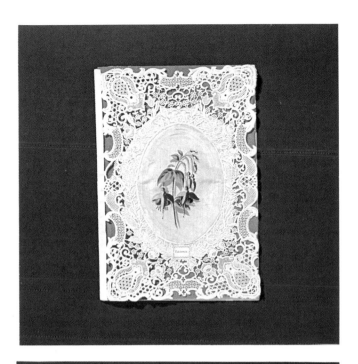

You're single now and pay attention,
To appointments gladly made,
Look beyond, – is your intention,
Thus to see a girl betrayed.

This "peep through the wedding ring" is an interesting little card. It shows the young bride of perhaps only a year or two's standing sitting forlornly and alone in the bedroom, her baby lying in the cot at her feet, and muttering bitterly: "not home yet & one o'clock." The card would seem hardly to express those sentiments that one would wish to convey to one's sweetheart, even were he erring. It is possible, however, that this card was designed for a completely different use; that it was the Victorian equivalent of the bawdy telegram sent to the bride and groom of a modern wedding. In this context it can be seen as a joke, none the less effective for its possible telling truth.

The style is reminiscent in places of the work of George Cruikshank or of Phiz. In the scene we see through the wedding ring the accent is on caricature and the lines simple and apparently careless. Far more attention to detail is evident in the scene below the ring where, with somewhat obscure symbolism, three cupids are reading from a book boldly titled "Love". Although the original etching was printed (black) the colouring of this card, as with many others, was added by hand, but here we have an example of just how crude such hand-colouring could sometimes be.

A PEEP THROUGH THE WEDDING RING.

You're single now and pay attention,
To appointments gladly made,
Look beyond,— is your intention,
Thus to see a girl betrayed.

This dainty little card has at its centre a printed scrap of white lilies – signifying "purity", "sweetness" and "modesty" in the Language of Flowers – surrounded by forget-me-nots. Further embossed paper forget-me-nots, at least some of them hand-painted, have been glued around this scrap, and also glued there are very fine coloured muslin flower shapes. The inscription, in crimson on a silver background, is in French although the card is in fact an English one. Written on the back of the card is the price, one shilling, but one cannot tell if this is original.

The embossing and perforation of the paper lace are unusually attractive, and a shell theme predominates. Perhaps the shell that is of most interest to us is the scallop, towards the lower right, with its close connections with Venus, the goddess of love.

Rather charmingly, the envelope bears a further testimony to the affection of the sender: the flap is embossed with a tiny figure of Cupid, on whose outstretched hand is perched a turtledove.

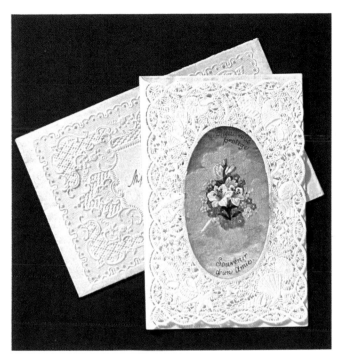

FORGET-ME-NOT

Sweet the bloom of affection's flower
*   Around our native cot,*
Which love in fancy's fairy hour,
*   First called "Forget-me-not!"*
Sweeter amid a farewell gloom
*   In our memory to spot,*
To foster in unfading bloom,
*   Love's flower, Forget-me-not.*

Give me a feeling faithful heart
Perfection's richest prize
This is a temple of all love
Where beauty never dies

reads the handwritten rhyme on this large card.
The card seems to have been bought by the donor
as a plain sheet with the embossed lace border, as
the flower and its surrounding decorations appear
to be hand-painted. The tulip – a variegated tulip
means, in the Language of Flowers, "beautiful
eyes" – is beautifully constructed of folded paper.
When she opened it up, the happy recipient could
see inside it a continuation of the design of blue
forget-me-nots tied with a silver bow.

FOND LOVE

Oh, never let thine eye grow cold,
Thy cherished voice grow rude
to me;
But let thy lip, as oft of old,
Still smile on me.

What more fitting sentiment than this with which
to end our voyage through a few of the oceans of
love?

Fond Love.

Oh, never let thine
eye grow cold,
Thy cherished
voice grow rude
to me;
But let thy lip, as oft
of old,
Still smile on me.

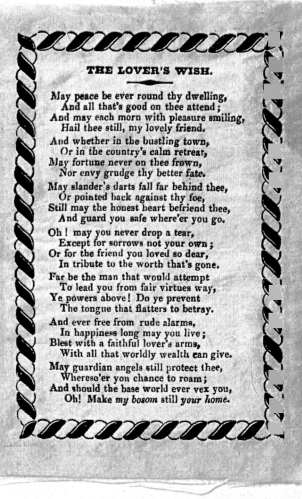

THE LOVER'S WISH.

May peace be ever round thy dwelling,
  And all that's good on thee attend;
And may each morn with pleasure smiling,
  Hail thee still, my lovely friend.

And whether in the bustling town,
  Or in the country's calm retreat,
May fortune never on thee frown,
  Nor envy grudge thy better fate.

May slander's darts fall far behind thee,
  Or pointed back against thy foe,
Still may the honest heart befriend thee,
  And guard you safe where'er you go.

Oh! may you never drop a tear,
  Except for sorrows not your own;
Or for the friend you loved so dear,
  In tribute to the worth that's gone.

Far be the man that would attempt
  To lead you from fair virtues way,
Ye powers above! Do ye prevent
  The tongue that flatters to betray.

And ever free from rude alarms,
  In happiness long may you live;
Blest with a faithful lover's arms,
  With all that worldly wealth can give.

May guardian angels still protect thee,
  Whereso'er you chance to roam;
And should the base world ever vex you,
  Oh! Make *my bosom* still *your home.*